Presented
by
Calvary Lutheran
Church

Baby in a Manger

Written by Julie Stiegemeyer

Illustrated by Nicole Wong

CONCORDIA PUBLISHING HOUSE · SAINT LOUIS

Unto the town of Nazareth,
    An angel brought God's Word.
A virgin girl of humble means
    The angel's message heard:

"You are the favored of the Lord,
    God's special chosen one.
For you will be the mother of
    God's one and only Son."

The angel's words confused the girl.
    "How can this be?" she said.
"How can I be a mother now,
    When I am not yet wed?"

"God's Holy Spirit will descend
And overshadow you.
Then in your womb will grow God's Son—
For God can all things do."

"I am the servant of the Lord,"
And Mary bowed her head.
"I will rejoice in God's great love.
May it be as you have said."

She rushed off to Elizabeth,
    Her cousin great with child,
Whose baby then heard Mary's voice
    And leaped; his mother smiled.

"My baby leaps for joy!" she cried.
    "Dear Mary, you are blessed!
You have believed God's precious Word!
    Please be my welcomed guest."

"The Mighty One has done great things,"
    Sang Mary, full of joy.
"His mercy will reach out to all
    Through my small baby boy!"

A man named Joseph worked with wood;
  He was a carpenter.
He loved dear Mary as his wife;
  He vowed to care for her.

But he could not quite understand
  God's great salvation plan.
Could Mary be the mother to
  Our God, come as a man?

Then one dark night while Joseph dreamed,
God's Word came to him too:
"This child of Mary's is God's Son.
And she'll be wife to you."

The angel spoke in Joseph's dream:
"This child will all men save.
Name this precious baby 'Jesus'—
The Savior that God gave."

Time passed; the baby grew and grew,
　　His birth day soon drew near.
But then the governor made a rule:
　　The law's decree was clear.

The government required that all
　　Must go to their hometown.
Although this changed the couple's plans,
　　They packed and then left town.

The donkey trotted carefully,
　　So precious was his load.
For on his back, the God of heav'n,
　　In Mary's womb was stowed.

Mary journeyed, tired and sore,
But tried not to complain.
She knew that God would care for her,
Even in her pain.

At last they came to Bethlehem,
So weary and forlorn,
And realized that it was time:
The child would soon be born.

So Joseph searched to find a room,
Or someplace with a bed,
But he could only find a home
For animals instead.

So animals were first to see,
Before it was yet morn.
There in the straw, among the beasts,
Our God in flesh was born.

Young Mary touched her little one,
Amazed at God's great love.
She wrapped her helpless babe in rags,
The Lord of heav'n above.

And angels sang a glorious song
    In shepherds' fields that night.
"All glory unto God above!"
    They sang in heavenly light.

Then to the stable shepherds ran
To see the baby boy,
To look upon the God of love,
Hearts filled with holy joy.

All knelt around the manger where
This baby in the straw
Lay helpless, but was God Himself.
They bowed in humble awe.

The shepherds, Mary, Joseph knew,
As they knelt down and prayed,
That on this day, God's mighty love
Through Jesus was displayed.

So may our hearts with joy delight
 In God's great gift of grace,
And look with faith upon our Lord,
 The holy Baby's face.

But may we also hold so dear
 The face of love and pain,
That from the cross forgave our sins,
 Eternal life to gain.

So may we race with shepherds' feet,
 To worship and adore,
To tell the world of God's great love
 And peace forevermore.

Today through water, bread, and wine
God takes away our sin.
A splash, a taste—God's love in Christ
To sinners comes again.

Published by Concordia Publishing House
3558 S. Jefferson Avenue
St. Louis, MO 63118-3968

Text copyright © 2004 Julie Stiegemeyer

Illustrations copyright © 2004 Concordia Publishing House

Manufactured in China

1 2 3 4 5 6 7 8 9 10   13 12 11 10 09 08 07 06 05 04

For
Glennis Hall and Sandra Stites,
Karen Anderson, Valerie Hale, and Kevann Cooke,
Tarah Roberts and Annie Heard,
with special thanks to
Mr. Gordon Brown
—D. J.

To Charnelle, with her growing doll collection
—M.C.P.

Henry Holt and Company, LLC
Publishers since 1866
115 West 18th Street
New York, New York 10011

Henry Holt is a registered trademark of Henry Holt and Company, LLC

Published in Canada by Fitzhenry & Whiteside Ltd.,
195 Allstate Parkway, Markham, Ontario L3R 4T8.

Library of Congress Cataloging-in-Publication Data
Johnson, Dinah.
Sitting pretty / Dinah Johnson; with photographs by Myles C. Pinkney.
Summary: A collection of photographs and poems celebrating black dolls from around the world;
includes historical background about some of the dolls.
1. Black dolls—Juvenile poetry. 2. Black dolls—Pictorial works. 3. Children's poetry,
American. [1. Black dolls—Poetry. 2. American poetry—Collections.]
I. Pinkney, Myles C., ill. II. Title.
PS3560.O3747 B45 2000 811'.54—dc21 99-49955

The author has made every effort to identify and credit the
designers or manufacturers of the dolls depicted in this book.
Please contact the publisher with any additions or corrections to the credits.

ISBN 0-8050-6097-9 / First Edition—2000
Printed in the United States of America on acid-free paper. ∞
1 3 5 7 9 10 8 6 4 2

Dinah Johnson

Sitting Pretty

A Celebration of Black Dolls

with photographs by
Myles C. Pinkney

Henry Holt and Company
New York

Introduction

Dolls are one of the special things that my editor, Christy Ottaviano, and I have in common. Long before this book came into being I'd seen pictures of her dolls and she'd seen snapshots of mine. I'm sure she understands the emptiness in the house when I packed up many of my dolls and sent them off to be photographed. The house wasn't the same without them. They and their personalities—gentle, joyful, bold—were absent from the walls and bookcases, the doors, beds, chests, and mantles, and were no longer flying from the fixtures. Made by women and men, out of cloth, wood, clay, metals, shells, paints, beads, the dolls remind me, and all who enter my home, of the beauty and imagination of human beings. Of course, they are not human. But they embody something of human creativity—our love of color and texture, our playfulness, our sense of self and being.

I grew up in a military family and my parents, the most wonderful in the world, bought me dolls from everywhere we visited. Even before I ever lived overseas myself, my father sent me dolls from Vietnam and Korea. I'm sure I got one in Iran. And I have them from all over Europe: Germany, Spain, Holland, Hungary. My father brought back figurines from Ethiopia after his first trip to the African continent; these were very special. I don't know exactly where all the dolls from my childhood are now. My guess is that they are in my parents' attic, living a life of their own.

The dolls I live with today, many of whom you'll meet in this book, are the dolls that came into my life when I was a grown-up. The combination doll, Katie-and-Cassie, was in my little Toyota Corolla when I began my drive, all alone, from South Carolina to California after finishing graduate school. I had found Katie-and-Cassie abandoned in an army-navy store in Charleston, in the heat of the summer. Thinking about it now, maybe this doll said something to me about where I came from and who I was becoming—a young professor interested in African-American studies, fascinated with how Africans refashioned their lives in their new homes.

In Oakland, I found Miss Clara Hazel and Charnelle. I went to several doll shows where I saw fancy dolls made by sophisticated dollmakers. I loved them. But I still loved cloth dolls best of all. And especially those dolls that friends gave me, as they did more often when they realized I was getting serious about collecting, about not being so alone in my tiny apartment but surrounded by visual and three-dimensional objects that give me strength. So my doll family kept growing. The dolls and poems in this book are divided into three sections that speak to the womanchild each of us recognizes in herself at different times in life.

I have many more dolls than could be included in this book. Two of the most dear to me are quite simple, made on bases of cardboard tubes, covered with fabric scraps, given to me by two women at a community center in Soweto, South Africa. Perhaps the other extreme is my Barbie doll. I love her sophistication and implied success in the modern world. But most important, I love the fact that she is not just Barbie colored brown. She represents an evolution in the history of American dolls that includes Beloved Belindy, the almost forgotten mammy doll in the Raggedy Ann stories. When I looked at my black Raggedy Ann dolls in writing about Precious, Lynn, and Elaine, I wondered what Beloved Belindy would say to her own daughters. I imagined her saying that no matter what the circumstances, no matter where we are in the African diaspora, if we know who we are, we can live with a dignity and spirit that never becomes raggedy.

This book is a celebration of women, children, doll artists, and their dolls, who are certainly not raggedy but, instead, sitting pretty. I don't mean that they are baby dolls sitting passively. They assume a certain stance and a certain attitude that will enable them to thrive in this world. They know their own minds and histories; they rejoice in their bodies and many kinds of beauty; they are comfortable with their voices and rhythms. My hope for my daughter, Niani, my niece Taelor Marie, and my nephew Richard is that they come to understand all of this. And I hope that these dolls and their words call readers into a place where everyone is—in the most meaningful way—sitting pretty.

Jumni

She has a little secret—
I can see it on
her lips
and in her eyes,
cutting to the side,
while she savors
her very own little secret
safely tucked inside
her heart.

Katie-and-Cassie

Katie lives in the big house;
Cassie lives in the cabin out back.
Katie picks pretty flowers;
Cassie totes cotton in a heavy sack.
Katie wants a doll for Christmas;
Cassie wants to learn to read.
Katie is free as a bird;
Cassie can only dream.

Precious, Lynn, and Elaine

Mama says, Don't be raggedy.
Be neat and tidy—
not raggedy.
Be kind and honest—
not raggedy.
Be curious and friendly,
smart and happy,
sassy and giving.
She says, Hold your heads high
and be who you are.
And you will never ever
be raggedy.

Tori Michelle

Tumbling in weave,
floating in fabric,
swimming in color—
   in motion,
   in color,
   in cloth . . .

   in motion,
   color,
   cloth.

Mocko

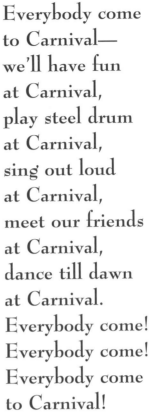

Everybody come
to Carnival—
we'll have fun
at Carnival,
play steel drum
at Carnival,
sing out loud
at Carnival,
meet our friends
at Carnival,
dance till dawn
at Carnival.
Everybody come!
Everybody come!
Everybody come
to Carnival!

Mariama, the African Mermaid

The mermaid makes her home
in places far and wide,
from one shore of the ocean
all the way to the other side.

Sometimes her home is Cameroon,
sometimes it's Charleston or St. Croix.
She is right at home wherever she finds
an African girl or boy.

Listen for the sound of the conch shell
wherever you may roam,
and you'll know the African mermaid
wants you to feel at home.

Charnelle

Charnelle is sitting pretty
in Grandma's high up bed.
Charnelle is sitting pretty
floating in perfume and lace.

Charnelle is sitting pretty
when she rests her sleepy head,
in a fluffy pillow
framing her pretty face.

Aunt Tilda

Dignified Miss Tilda
is our neighbor
and she's our teacher too
in our little one-room school
down the way.

Serious Miss Tilda
makes us work—
reading, writing, arithmetic, and recitation—
it's work, work, work, no play,

until she becomes
our laughing Aunt Tilda again
when we leave school
at the end of the day.

Ailea and James Julian

Mommy can't find me
when I'm lost inside a book.

Daddy can call my name
and call again,
but he doesn't know where to look.

Because we could be just about anywhere
in the whole wide world,
meeting other boys and girls
who are lost inside a book.

Big Sister's Dolls

Tera

Her hair is a sculpture
as wild as the wind.

Her arms are the beat
of the earth's own drum.

Her voice is the song
of the oldest stars.

Her face is the moon
and the sun.

Mahari

Shooting
color
across the night sky—
high.

Streaking
color
through the night air—
up there.

Flying
color
is the night star—
afar.

Girl!
You

Ashley and Quinnie

Ashley and Quinnie
meet each afternoon
to drink their sassafras tea.

They paint sometimes
and they read sometimes,
then they drink their sassafras tea.

They write poems that rhyme
and dream and scheme
while they drink their sassafras tea.

They promise each other
they will always be friends
and raise a toast with their sassafras tea.

Imani Dawn

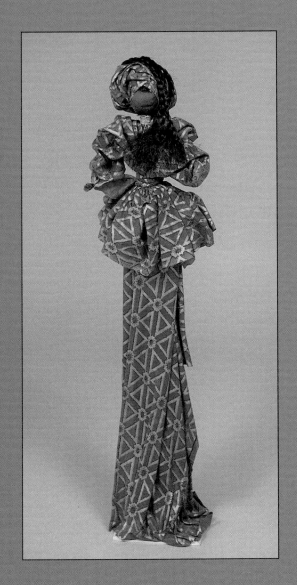

Tall
like a tree.
Straight
like a tree.
Strong,
Rooted,
Inviting,
like a tree.
Silent
like a tree.
Singing
like a tree.
Reaching up,
Lovely,
Ancient,
like a tree.

Jasmine, Kendra, and Nia

Walk across the bridge—
the stream is not so very wide—
take one step then another
until you reach the other side.

Walk across the bridge—
it's not so hard to do—
look straight ahead and don't turn back,
your sisters are waiting for you.

Desmond and Shalaine

Nobody can make me laugh
like my brother.
Every day.

Nobody can make me feel better
like my sister.
In her special way.

Nobody else is Desmond.
Nobody else is Shalaine.

Shona and Sing

Shona's beads
tell the history
of her family.

Sing's dress
tells the history
of her family.

The wise things they said
in bands of red,
each band of gold
a promise to hold,
every band of color
for a sister or a mother—
circles of fathers
and cousins and brothers.
Each band of green
is for the land they loved,
brown for their eyes
looking down from above.

Shona's dress
is a celebration
of generations
of the Zulu nation.

Sing's beads
are a celebration
of generations
of the Seminole nation.

Eboni and Kiana

Earth black
Sister black
Midnight black
Singing black
Rich black
Strong black
Blue black
True black

Sonia

Move out of my way, mister.
I've places to go—
I have my bag and I'm on my way.

'Scuse me, ma'am.
I must walk steady—
I haven't time to dally today.

Scat now, chi'ren.
I have important things to do—
I cannot stop to play.

Sierra

Isn't my mommy beautiful
with a baby in her belly?

Isn't my mommy beautiful
walking down the beach?

So happy
she's so happy.

Isn't my mommy beautiful
toting baskets full of fruit?

Mommy says yes, she feels special,
because her life is full
of love and work and play
and children.

So happy
she's so happy.

Niani

You are the power
of purple and gold,

full of energy
set to explode,

always loving and joyful
and smart and bold.

Shakhlan

In my heart you're not a stranger to me,
so I call you my sister across the sea.
Though I can't speak your language
and you can't speak mine,
the words we want will come in time.
And for right now our hearts will speak,
mine to you and yours to me—
    through laughter,
    through kindness,
    through touch.

Shirl, Justice, and Deb

Marching steady,
strong like metal,
arms together,
we will bend—
we will not break.

Marching steady,
fists like fire,
we will overcome—
someday.

Miss Clara Hazel

Red ripe apples!
Buy my fine fat apples!
Luscious, juicy, sweet!

You can bake them in pies.
You can dip them in caramel.
Or bob them in a barrel for a treat.

Red ripe apples!
Buy my fine fat apples!
You will find nothing better to eat!

Desiree, Audrey, Sharon, and Judith

Desiree comes with gumbo;
she's from Louisiana.

Audrey cooked some blackcake;
she is from Guyana.

Sharon can throw down some fried chicken,
the best of Alabama.

Judith from Jamaica
brings breadfruit and banana.

Friends sharing supper
sharing love.

Miss Frona

Sitting every week
on the very first pew—
proper and pretty
in her suit of blue
and white lace—
she wouldn't be caught
without a magnificent hat
and a flower picked fresh
from her garden.

Inezzi

Her face is turned
toward AFRICA
over there.

She lifts her arms
as if she's going to fly back
over there.

Her body is in the New World
but her heart is already
over there.

She whispers,
by and by we will meet
at HOME back
over there.

Retta

She wears a crown of color
open like a fan,
surprising as a rainbow,
an umbrella
of magic
and memory.

Dahomé Kalena

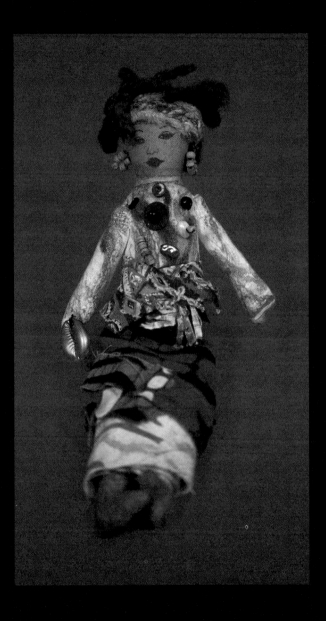

Earth woman
Water woman
Wild woman
Proud woman
Spirit woman
Real woman
Night woman
Day woman
Black woman
Purple woman
Yesterday today
Tomorrow woman
Head woman
Heart woman
Girl woman
Grown woman
Woman

Author's Notes

Jumni: My sister Debora brought me this doll from Cameroon, West Africa, in 1994. Jumni is named for the daughter of our family friends Benn and Agnes Bongang. Her hair is skillfully braided and her red shoes are real leather. She carries a baby on her back.

Katie-and-Cassie: I bought this topsy-turvy doll in Charleston, South Carolina. This kind of doll can take many forms. Red Riding Hood and the Wolf is another topsy-turvy combination I've seen.

Precious, Lynn, and Elaine: The doll with the curly brown hair was given to me by my friend Elaine Nichols and was made by Carrie Coachman, a noted quilter and dollmaker on Pawley's Island, South Carolina. The small one in the green dress was a gift from my friend Sharon Bryant.

Tori Michelle was a gift to my daughter, Niani, from Jim Lacy. The border of her colorful dress is trimmed with lace and she wears dainty lace petticoats.

Mocko: This Mocko Jumbie doll was designed by Henry Leonard. I bought it in Atlanta, but it represents a figure that is a very important part of Carnival in the Virgin Islands.

Mariama was found at a flea market, wearing denim overalls. I re-dressed her and wrapped her head in mud cloth and added earrings of cowrie shells and brass.

Charnelle is "Kizzy" from Arnett's Country Store. I bought Charnelle in Oakland, California, in 1988. I love her bonnet and expressive eyes. She's named for the daughter of *Sitting Pretty*'s photographer, Myles C. Pinkney.

Aunt Tilda was made by T. Jones of North Carolina. I love the details of the eyeglasses around her neck and the boy holding the Holy Bible. [Copyright © 1993 by Artful Presentations.]

Ailea and James Julian: These sculpted and glazed dolls are the work of B. Grice. They were a gift to Niani from Karen Starks.

Tera was bought in Columbia, South Carolina, and was made by Anne Mayer Meier of Daphne, Alabama. Her wire hair and other features make her seem both ancient and new.

Mahari was made by dollmaker Pat Flynn. Her red straw halo is glorious. She was a gift from LaVeta Small.

Glennis: This Barbie, "In the Limelight," was designed by the African-American designer Byron Lars. He attended to every detail, even her diamond ring. [BARBIE is a trademark owned and used under license from Mattel, Inc. © 1999 Mattel, Inc. All rights reserved. BARBIE® fashion designed by Byron Lars, under license. BARBIE® doll image used with permission.]

Ashley and Quinnie: Quinnie was bought at an antique shop in Brooklyn, New York. She is said to have had only one owner for the past sixty-five years. Ashley was rescued at a New York City flea market for seven dollars. Both dolls, part of my editor's collection, are composition molds (made from a mixture of wood, pulp, plaster, and glue) and were manufactured in America between 1920 and 1940.

Imani Dawn was the creation of Philadelphia dollmaker Lorrie Payne [copyright © 1997].

Jasmine, Kendra, and Nia: The tall doll was a gift from Lynette Robinson, brought from Ghana. Notice her carefully braided hair. I don't know the origin of the others, but their details are striking: embroidered facial features and movable arms on the one with the white headtie, and broomwhisk skirt on the other one holding the baby on her back.

Candace, "She Who Claims the Story," is by Ninae/Tamu Imani Doll. She is made from fabric that was meticulously wrapped, hand-painted, then shellacked.

Douglas and Beatrice: Douglas is actually Reverend Johnson of the Daddy's Long Legs company [copyright © 1991]. Beatrice is Esther of that same company [copyright © 1993]. I've renamed them after my parents, Douglas and Beatrice Taylor Johnson.

Farah: This doll was made by Serena Mann of Seattle, Washington. She is papier-mâché with wrapped fabric that is shellacked.

Vashti and Gina: I think that the tall doll is from Namibia in southern Africa. She was purchased in the Disneyland gift shop. The small doll was found at a shop in South Carolina. She's probably from the West Indies.

Desmond and Shalaine: These dolls are constructed on a T-base with wooden heads. The cowrie shell on Shalaine's dress was once used as currency but is now used as decoration and as a symbol of the power of the oceans.

Shona and Sing: The beaded doll is a traditional one from the Zulu/Ndebele nation of southern Africa. The dress of zigzag appliqués is Seminole (Native American). Her head is a kind of small gourd, similar to a coconut. She was found at a flea market by my friend, folklorist Lesley Williams.

Eboni and Kiana: Eboni, with the pointed hat, was given to me by Candace Smith, who bought her during her first trip to the Motherland, in 1997, at age eight. Kiana was another gift to me.

Sonia: My sister-in-law, Sonia King-Johnson, brought this doll to me from her native Barbados, West Indies. The earrings are made from a bean and the shoulder bag is woven with plant fiber.

Sierra was made by Meykal [copyright © 1996]. Her jewelry is exquisite and the fruit in her bucket looks almost real. Her hair is the texture of authentic dreadlocks. There are feathers in her headdress.

Niani was bought in Brooklyn, New York. The fabric of her dress is reminiscent of Ghanaian Adinkra cloth, the symbols of which carry significance [copyright © 1992, 1993 by Kathryn Simmons].

Shakhlan was purchased in Cape Town, South Africa, in 1996.

Shirl, Justice, and Deb: I bought this doll in Harlem. It was made by California jewelry artist Christine Olmstead. Two inches high, this piece is made of metal, fiber, and plastic. Arms upraised, the three figures that make up the one pin remind me of the brave marchers in the United States civil rights struggle.

Miss Clara Hazel: I bought Hazel in Oakland in 1988. She is named for a friend who loves gardening. If you look closely, you'll see apples in her bucket.

Desiree, Audrey, Sharon, and Judith: These dolls are named for my friends who really are from the places named in the poem—Louisiana, Alabama, Guyana, and Jamaica. The tall one toting the basket on her head is the most unique: she has a cloth face but her arms and legs are wooden.

Miss Frona: This is in the Daddy's Long Legs series, but I'm not sure which one. She was a gift from my friend Dr. Sandra Stites. I love Miss Frona partly because she is dressed identically to my grandmother in one of my cherished photographs of her.

Inezzi was made by celebrated dollmaker Marcella Welch [copyright © 1987, #302]. She is a cloth doll whose dress is made from hand-painted fabric.

Retta is an Akuaba doll from Ghana, West Africa, of the Akan civilization. She is the queen of all dolls of the African diaspora, representing fertility and the life force of our people.

Dahomé Kalena was made by Marcella Welch and was bought in Atlanta in 1996. Her purple hair is fiber, her bodice is covered with buttons, and she's holding a gold-painted cowrie shell.

Malaika [on back cover] was a gift to my niece Taelor Marie Johnson. Her origin is unknown.